HAUS CURIOSITIES

Establishment and Meritocracy

In memory of Michael Foot

1919–2012

Historian, soldier, friend, mentor
and connoisseur of secret establishments

About the Author

Peter Hennessy is Attlee Professor of Contemporary British History at Queen Mary, University of London. He was educated at Marling School, Stroud; St John's College, Cambridge; the London School of Economics and Harvard (where he was a Kennedy Scholar 1971–72). He spent 20 years in journalism with spells on *The Times*, the *Financial Times* and *The Economist* and as a presenter of the BBC Radio 4 *Analysis* programme. He is a Fellow of the British Academy and sits as an independent crossbench peer in the House of Lords as Lord Hennessy of Nympsfield.

Peter Hennessy

ESTABLISHMENT AND MERITOCRACY

HAUS
CURIOSITIES

First published by Haus Publishing in 2014
70 Cadogan Place
London SW1X 9AH
www.hauspublishing.com

Copyright © Peter Hennessy, 2014

The right of the author to be identified as the author
of this work has been asserted in accordance with
the Copyright, Designs and Patents Act 1988

A CIP catalogue record for this book is
available from the British Library

Print ISBN: 978-1-908323-77-4
Ebook ISBN: 978-1-908323-78-1

Typeset in Garamond by MacGuru Ltd
info@macguru.org.uk

Printed in Spain

Prologue

There were multiple triggers for this pamphlet. First, my long and much valued friendship with Barbara Schwepcke of Haus Publishing. Second, our conversation during the Haus 10th anniversary dinner at the Reform Club in London on 16 February 2013. That night Barbara and I regretted the passing, outside the think tank world, of pamphlets on topical themes which was so powerful a strand of politico-literary life in the interwar years especially within the yellow-orange covers of Victor Gollancz's celebrated Left Book Club (though the Gollancz oeuvre was usually rather bigger than pamphlets). The idea of the Haus Curiosities – a homage to Einstein's great dictum 'Never lose a holy curiosity' – developed from that evening at the Reform and in November 2013 over lunch in the House of Lords the deal was struck whereby I am now putting pen to paper on Haus Curiosity No.1.

In the meantime there had been other triggers for this squib which did not always involve lunching or dining in Establishment service stations of various kinds – though an after dinner speech on 'The Establishment' to the benchers of the Middle Temple in May 2013 was certainly one of them.[1] In the autumn of 2013 I delivered further thoughts on 'The British Establishment' to the Inside Out Festival at the Royal Society of Arts and a lecture on 'Meritocracy Revisited', the theme of the Michael Young Family and Kinship Memorial

Lecture 2013 which I was invited to deliver by Grandparents Plus at the Royal Society of Medicine. In January 2014 I spoke, too, at the Harkness Fellows' Annual Dinner on 'The Idea of a British Establishment'. I was fortunate also to be invited by the Lord Mayor of London, Roger Gifford, to take part in his symposium on 'The Authority of Institutions: Symbolism and Change' at the Mansion House in October 2013.

I was very grateful to the Middle Temple, the Inside Out Festival, Grandparents Plus and the Harkness Fellows for their combined stimuli to revisit the interlocking themes of Establishment and Meritocracy. 'Revisit' was the right verb because such speculations had intrigued me over several decades. For they were – and are – very much a part of the intellectual compost that made my generation of young postwar Brits who were good at exams. The Establishment notion and the concept of a spreading, growing and eventually self-propelling meritocracy was bound to intrigue people like me who benefitted mightily from climbing the postwar ladders of opportunity. What, for example, were state and local authority funded grants to an expanding number of students designed to do? It was plain enough. To get the young and gifted into higher education whatever the socio-economic position of their parents. What were universities for if not to enable a meritocracy to rise?

Anatomising and analysing the twin themes of Establishment and Meritocracy is a huge undertaking that deserves a big book. This volume is not it. It is not even an executive summary-style surrogate for the big book. It's more the thoughts I would offer the brave young social and political historian if he or she came to see me for a chat before setting out on the stretching task of mapping and analysing these most potent yet highly elusive phenomena.

Peter Hennessy
Walthamstow, Westminster, Sheffield and
South Ronaldsay, April 2014

Contents

The Twin Themes

Our very British preoccupation, generation after generation, with the idea of an 'Establishment' suggests that within a good number of us there lurks an amateur social anthropologist fuelled by an ancient urge clothed in modern form to divine who are the elders of the tribes and the institutions that matter to us. The professional anthropologist, Mary Douglas, caught something of this in her *How Institutions Think* when she observed that 'writing about cooperation and solidarity means writing at the same time about rejection and mistrust'.[2]

Here we find one of the crossover points to the concept of meritocracy. For the preoccupation with merit, I think, is linked to this – the wish, the almost indignant expectation that those who make it into the Establishment enclosure are propelled there by their abilities and powers of application rather than shimmering in thanks to birth or social connection. Establishments are irritating enough to those who feel excluded or patronised by them without the unmeritorious blagging or breeding their way into their ranks. As a result the notion of Establishment will always be twinned with the concept of meritocracy not least perhaps because in many people's eyes merit tempers privilege. The same applies to the honours system, a phenomenon which needs at least a pamphlet to capture its contemporary cartography and the degree to which it reflects Britain in the 2010s. It's intriguing, for example, to note that at the very apex of the honours system there sits the lustrous Order of Merit. It was founded by Edward VII in 1902. Its numbers are restricted to 24 and appointments are made personally by the Monarch.[3]

Perhaps the best way to imagine the twinned themes is as a pair of trains running on parallel tracks throughout postwar society taking on extra passengers and baggage by the decade. One of the reasons both the Establishment and the Meritocracy expresses have fascinated me is that, to some extent, I have been a passenger on both. And one of the more compelling aspects of writing the history of one's own times is that desire to make sense of its autobiographical elements.

Over the four decades of which I have been conscious of them, I have carried in my mind a certain idea of the pair. Meritocracy is the clearer of the two – the notion that the gifted and the energetic rise in terms of professions and rewards (in terms of both salary and wider status) on the basis of demonstrable merit whatever the social and financial positions of their families rather than because of inherited wealth or family connections.

Establishment is fuzzier – a phantom army of the great and good who fill positions in public, cultural and intellectual life exercising a special kind of subtle, supple, concealed soft power within our institutions and our society. Its members can set the tone, influence the direction of public policy and exert considerable sway over future appointments to the professions within which they have risen. Yet plenty of successful people would be appalled to think they were Establishment figures. It is not a label for flaunting. Indeed many would define themselves against it. Though quite often they quietly slip inside it during their middle and later years while remaining determined not to succumb to its state-of-mind, which is itself the mistiest of concepts.

Despite this myriad of ethereal qualities, the Establishment has brought much joy and humour as the perfect tethered goat for satirists. This has been particularly true since the early 1960s when that genius among satirists, Peter Cook, founded The Establishment Club in Soho for the purposes of nightly lampooning amidst the rich opportunities presented by the Conservative government of Harold Macmillan as it proceeded to decay like a ripe stilton.

Establishments in various forms will always be with us. And here, in my view, one finds the bonding – the twinning – with meritocracy. If we have to have an Establishment, let it be a meritorious one. And yet, as we shall see shortly, there are problems carried aboard that express train marked 'meritocracy' – some undesirable fellow travellers whose *mentalités* can lead to unwanted destinations.

A number of sub-themes will arise in the course of the pages to come as well as touches of history to illustrate the continuing allure of the two notions. Do they – have they – had a use as explainers of important aspects of British society and institutions? Why do they appeal, in one form or another, to those who seek to label groups, individuals, trends? To what extent are they both imagined concepts? And, perhaps most difficult of all, did a British meritocracy rise despite the, of late, disappointing trajectory of social mobility? But first to the 1950s and 1960s – to the popular revival of the word 'Establishment' and the creation of an entirely new one, 'meritocracy'.

Revival and Rise

It was in the 1950s that the two themes started to fizz. In the early part of the decade, the historian AJP Taylor and the political commentator Henry Fairlie revived the idea of a shadowy yet potent British Establishment which exerted an ill-defined and intangible yet real effect in public, political and cultural life. Writing at much the same time, the historical sociologist Michael Young was working on his *The Rise of the Meritocracy*[4] which, given the surprising difficulty he encountered in finding a publisher, did not reach the shelves until 1958, and eventually the pages of the dictionaries as a new social category-cum-concept.

'Establishment' is a slippery term but it's everywhere. When used incontinently, it's easy to wonder if Establishment exists as more than a notion, a convenient piece of linguistic litter to deploy as a weapon of disdain, even denunciation, against individuals or clusters of people who you don't care for, rather resent and wish to annoy.

Indeed, to declare an interest, if the British Establishment does exist, part of me must be part of it. Why? I like clubs, especially the dining variety. I have a fondness for traditional institutions and, when Parliament is sitting, spend a good part of the week in the House of Lords, which many might see as the Establishment's debating chamber, canteen, chat show and retirement home all folded into one. Gabriele

Annan, wife of Lord Annan, famously used to describe it as 'Noel's playgroup'.[5]

The Establishment notion does matter because, generation upon generation, so many intelligent and not always so intelligent people have thought it does exist – though the form it takes mutates and is always and everywhere immensely stretching to capture and define. As Jeremy Paxman, who wrote a good book about it in 1991 called *Friends in High Places*, puts it:

> It is a harlot of a word, convenient, pliant, available for a thousand meaningless applications.[6]

Yet there exists a widespread sense of the Establishment as an inner track of people who fix things discreetly, unavowedly and unaccountably behind carefully painted camouflage giving it a whiff of genteel conspiracy perhaps even with a dash of insider trading in the influence market.

It's a concept that has stalked me for the bulk of my working life and, in return, I have stalked it, especially when I wrote about Whitehall for *The Times* in the 1970s and 1980s. In the mid-1970s, for example, the incomparable David Butler introduced me to his seminar on British government and politics at Nuffield College, Oxford as 'The gossip columnist of the British Establishment'. I was faintly irritated by this at the time – but had to admit there was something in it.

I acquired my first notion of the British Establishment by reading Anthony Sampson's second *Anatomy of Britain Today* published in 1965[7] which I received as a sixth-form prize at Marling School, my grammar school in Stroud,

Gloucestershire. In his first edition of 1962, Sampson set out to find it across a huge range of British institutions and professions. He reached an intriguing conclusion. Not only did he dismiss conspiracy theory, he declared that:

> My own fear is not that the 'Establishment' in Britain is too close, but that it is not close enough, that the circles are overlapping less and less, and that one half of the ring has very little contact with the other half. In particular, the hereditary Establishment of interlocking families, which still has an infectious social and political influence on the Conservative Party, banking and many industries, has lost touch with the new worlds of science, industrial management and technology, and yet tries to apply old amateur ideals into technical worlds where they won't fit.[8]

Sampson's thinking was very much a pre-echo of the theme Harold Wilson made his own when he became Leader of the Labour Party in 1963.

Ben Pimlott, Wilson's biographer, describing his 'New Britain' sequence of speeches in 1964 which Wilson hoped would catapult him into Downing Street in the general election that year (they did; just[9]), wrote that 'The attack was not on the abstraction "capitalism", but on the undiscerning, inefficient, backward-looking better off. Instead of aristocracy and plutocracy there would be classless meritocracy, "a Britain in which the Government picks the best brains in the land and harnesses them to the task of national regeneration"'.[10] 'Ability', Wilson liked to say, 'must be the test, and ability is not to be measured by upper-class accents'.[11]

Meritocracy, should it rise, would be the transcender – perhaps even the banisher – of class. In the interim it would, in Wilson's hands, serve as a tidy weapon of politically-charged class warfare.

Anthony Sampson in his 1960s 'Anatomies' was drawing, too, on that Fifties revival of the Establishment notion by the powerful pens – of AJP Taylor and Henry Fairlie. Taylor took up the theme in what was then still called *The New Statesman and Nation* in August 1953 in a review of a new life of William Cobbett,[12] agriculturalist, journalist and a great denouncer of the Establishment which he called 'The Thing'. Taylor's opening paragraph remains, I think, a collector's item. 'Trotsky', he began,

> tells how, when he first visited England, Lenin took him round London and, pointing out the sights, exclaimed: 'That's *their* Westminster Abbey! That's *their* Houses of Parliament!'... By *them* he meant not the English, but the governing classes, the Establishment. And indeed in no other European country is the Establishment so clearly defined and so complacently secure.[13]

Henry Fairlie's assault on the British Establishment in his *Spectator* column was triggered by the Foreign Office, then seen as an Establishment pinnacle, finally admitting in September 1955 that two of their own diplomats, Guy Burgess and Donald Maclean, who had disappeared in May 1951, were, in fact, Soviet spies and were now living in Moscow.[14] Fairlie convinced himself that the long, if now-broken, official silence was an example of 'the "Establishment" at work' and by 'Establishment' he meant not 'only the centres of official power – though they are certainly part of it – but rather the whole matrix of official and social relations within which power is exercised'.[15]

Such matrices are very difficult to trace. In the mid-1980s I tried to pin down at least part of the Establishment matrix when I wrote a pamphlet for the Policy Studies Institute called *The Great and the Good: An Inquiry into the British Establishment*.[16] My cunning plan was to trace the tribe that had peopled the Royal Commissions and Committees of Inquiry since the Second World War and to pen mini-biographies of a trio of outstanding princes of greatness and goodness – the civil servant and wartime Home Secretary, John Anderson, the great jurist Cyril Radcliffe and the philosopher and public administrator Oliver Franks,[17] grand inquirers all, whose recommendations always carried great weight, even if they were not accepted in full. But influence is the Establishment's hard currency.

This was a promising approach at the time but soon became less so as successive governments rather gave up on Royal Commissions and Committees of Inquiry, reaching for task forces, czars, focus groups and relying on the newer think-tanks of varying quality that bloomed in the late Seventies and early Eighties. There is still some mileage in this approach. As my friend and former student Dr Rosaleen Hughes has pointed out, there remain individuals who are called upon by the state to perform duties beyond the professions in which they have made their names. Judges are the most obvious example but, as Rosaleen noted, it applies to business people brought in to inquire such as our mutual friend John Browne, Lord Browne of Madingley, on the funding of students in higher education.

Tracing who influences policy, in what way and when is always difficult however, even when the archives are opened. In a strange way this adds still more to the mystery and mystique of the Establishment.

A New Landscape?

Henry Fairlie's article was succeeded a few years later by two other collectors' items for the pursuer of Establishment studies. First the 1959 'symposium', *The Establishment*, edited by the then 27 year-old Hugh Thomas, to which Henry Fairlie contributed an essay on the BBC.[18] Hugh Thomas resigned from the Foreign Office over the Suez affair in 1956 (and went on to write a very good book about it[19] and a classic work on the Spanish Civil War[20]) and now sits on the crossbenches as Lord Thomas of Swynnerton.

Hugh Thomas' attempt at a historical geography of the Establishment depicted it as a civilian equivalent of the Brigade of Guards (my image, not his) protecting the equally elusive British constitution:

> The Establishment, briefly, is the English constitution, and the group of institutions and outlying agencies built round it to assist in its protection; it naturally also includes all those who stand like commissionaires before these protective institutions to protect *them*. The word derives, of course, from the ecclesiastical establishment of the Anglican church ...[21]

So what was it that the young Hugh Thomas saw the Establishment girding itself to protect in the late 1950s?

Now it is ... Victorian England, with all its prejudices, ignorances and inhibitions, that the Establishment sets out to defend. The Establishment is the present-day institutional museum of Britain's past greatness.[22]

And the youthful Thomas cited the public schools (anatomised in the symposium by John Vaizey,[23] the educational economist who also fetched up in the House of Lords) as a prime example providing 'a continuous stream of socially gifted and athletic amateurs to act as proconsuls in, however, an Empire that no longer exists in 1959'.[24]

Fifty-five years on I asked Hugh Thomas how he would depict the Establishment in 2014? He replied:

You asked me about the current membership of the so-called Establishment. I told you that I did not think that it exists in the old sense. If it did so, surely I would have been elected a member long ago. The tie would be hanging in my wardrobe. The membership fees would have been annually released from my bank. The reunions would have been attended. And ... I should have had the anthem (we would not have called it a song) by heart 'Olim fuit ...'[25]

Three years after the Thomas symposium and about the time the first Sampson *Anatomy of Britain* appeared, Kingsley Martin, the then fabled editor of *The New Statesman*, opened up a new front on the long march in search of the British Establishment. Martin tried the tack of asking who was the head of it? For him, in his *The Crown and The*

Establishment,[26] the answer was as obvious as it was simple – the Monarch. And how does the King or Queen of the day sustain the role of Keeper of the Establishment as if it were the unacknowledged twin of Defender of the Faith? Through that ancient monarchical device of the Privy Council, that's how.

'In a fluid society', wrote Kingsley Martin,

> which is based on a parliamentary and representative system, the Prime Minister and his senior colleagues are inevitably incorporated into the Establishment. One way of ensuring that an influential politician will not revolt against it is to make him a Privy Councillor; the Leader of the Opposition is in effect co-opted by receiving a substantial salary. The Monarch plays an essential part in holding this system together. He or she is the one person to whom all intimate quarrels and controversies at the top, officially secret level may legitimately be made known. Either personally or through private secretaries, the Monarchy is the depository of much highly confidential information, and it may be its job to smooth out disharmonies within the Establishment. The Monarchy may act as the final arbiter when there appears danger of a breach in the continuity of government.[27]

This argument is a mixture of fact and fantasy. The Queen certainly was in a delicate position during the transition from Harold Macmillan to Alec Douglas-Home in No.10 Downing Street a year after Kingsley Martin's book appeared, in the days when Conservative leaders 'emerged' without resort to a ballot of Tory MPs.[28] But to imply, as the Martin thesis does, that but for their privy councillorships or salaries Ramsay MacDonald, Clement Attlee, Hugh Gaitskell or, a year later, Harold Wilson might have wished to remake the British state in a fundamentally radical fashion or were prevented from pushing through heavy-duty socialist measures because they had the letters 'PC' after their names is absurd – all the more so because Kingsley Martin knew these men.

To be sure, a touch of monarchical stardust which in the mid-nineteenth century Walter Bagehot thought essential to its mystique ('when there is a select committee on the Queen the charm of royalty will be gone. Its mystery is its life. We must not let in daylight upon magic'[29]) clung to the reign of Queen Elizabeth II in the early 1960s (certainly far more than today though the Queen is still powerful box office). Anthony Sampson recognised this in his 1962 *Anatomy* when he wrote that 'in many of the conflicts that appear in this book – between old schools and new, old universities and new, classicists and scientists, public service and trade, old regiments and new corps, the royal magic hangs always over the old'.[30]

I have, however, a dash of sympathy for anyone who tries to depict the undepictable, to catch the essence or the crewing of the British Establishment at any particular moment in its wraith's progress. Any attempt is likely to look either naïve or way off or both to those who came later. My own mid-1980s attempt to find them amongst the postwar Good and Great certainly does. The 'Czars' and 'Task Forces' that have in part replaced Royal Commissions have not produced *grand corps* comparable to that exhibited by the great inquirers of the past. And the Establishment concept has been made still more elusive over the past quarter-of-a-century by the rise of a new political economy (the post-Big Bang City, hedge funds and all that) plus an electronic media explosion driven by new technologies alongside the grander newspapers not to mention the new Britain, young country again banalities of 'New Labour' which held the field and tempted the credulous (as did something I could never grasp called the 'Third Way'[31]) for a few years after 1997.

Such *non*-Establishment developments intrigued me afresh in April 2013. The first occasion was when Jonathan Hill, Lord Hill of Oareford, the Leader of the House of Lords, opened the tributes to Lady Thatcher by recalling 1975 when, as Jonathan put it, 'this non-establishment figure had become leader of the establishment party'.[32] A couple of weeks later I was talking with a man I hugely admire, a scientist and a member of the House of Lords who has run top-of-the-range institutions and yet has that modesty and quietness that can go with great scientists.[33] If there were league tables for Establishment and meritocracy he would be at the very top of the Premiership in both.

I asked him if a British Establishment still existed. 'I don't believe there is such a thing as "The Establishment"', he said. 'If Anthony Sampson went looking for it now he would find it completely different – in the hedge funds; in the media; the sort of people who would think that academia and the clubs are the *ancien régime*'.

My greatly admired friend set me thinking. I reckon there is a permanent element at the core of the British Establishment – a kind of gyroscope – which embraces the grand old professions like the Law and the Civil Service (though the latter is a tad tattered at the moment), the House of Lords (especially sections of the crossbenches where sit the former Cabinet Secretaries, Law Lords, Chiefs of the Defence Staff and Queen's Private Secretaries), the Royal Society, the British Academy, the learned societies generally, the scientific and engineering institutes and the great medical colleges. The reach and clout of these institutions and tribes may fluctuate but they never truly fade, let alone disappear. While around this rooted, inner core there swirl the transient elements in the media, the financial world and the celebritocracy in constellations that vary from generation to generation who can have a powerful, if often passing influence on the mood music of political and economic discussion, and in the case of celebritocracy, the norms of our wider society. If I were writing that book on the British Establishment the permanent/temporary divide would govern my approach.

A Secret Establishment?

If there is such a thing as a truly inner core to the British Establishment protected by the most carefully constructed barriers, where might we find it? Could it be the interlocking worlds of the secret state, the intelligence and security services in particular? It was a former Chief of the Defence Staff who in conversation in 2013 wondered how somebody (not himself) 'got through the Establishment filters'.[34] The secret world undoubtedly has several sub-sets of those filters that are peculiarly its own and, once navigated, are marked by an unspoken initiation rite, what Rachel Ward called in another context, 'the precious language of belonging: gossip'.[35]

In any book-length study of the British Establishment an attempt would need to be made to penetrate this aspect of its secret anthropologies. And I would start with the man who has shaped British perceptions of that strange, perpetually fascinating world – John le Carré. He has the keenest eye for social origins and here is how he introduces his readers to the background of the greatest of his creations in *Call for the Dead*, published in 1961. It's a social treatise and a testament to, in Smiley's case, meritocracy in a single, beautifully constructed sentence:

And so Smiley, without school, parents, regiment or trade,

without wealth or property, travelled without labels in the guard's van of the social express.[36]

The secret world are keen readers of le Carré. And, occasionally, one hears internal echoes of him.

This is particularly true of what the insiders tend to think of (as I do) as his greatest novel, *Tinker, Tailor, Soldier, Spy*.[37] A trio of examples. The 'Circus" greatest KGB-watcher, Connie Sachs, in drink-laden and embittered enforced retirement by the intelligence leadership that has fallen wholesale for a huge Russian deception in 'Source Merlin', has an eloquently revealing emotional spasm when Smiley is about to take leave of her after a visit to raid her still formidable mind about a senior Russian intelligence officer, Aleksey Polyakov, operating under diplomatic cover out of the Soviet Embassy in London.

> 'Poor loves.' She was breathing heavily, not perhaps from any one emotion but from a whole mess of them, washed around in her liked mixed drinks. 'Poor loves. Trained to Empire, trained to rule the waves. All gone. All taken away. Bye-bye world. You're the last George, you and Bill. And filthy Percy a bit'. He had known it would end like this; but not quite so awfully.[38]

Nearly 20 years after Le Carré's 1974 classic, one of the Queen's Private Secretaries was lunching at the real 'Circus' – the headquarters of the Secret Intelligence Service, MI6, at its old location in South London, Century House, just down the road from Lambeth North tube station. As he took his leave he inquired of his hosts, 'What shall I tell Her Majesty her Secret Intelligence Service is for?' 'Please tell her', replied Sir Gerry Warner, the SIS Deputy Chief, 'it is the last penumbra of her Empire'.[39]

Second example. Towards the end of *Tinker Tailor Soldier Spy* Smiley visits the now-unmasked traitor in detention awaiting despatch to Russia in an exchange deal with Moscow. The mole engages in 'a long apologia' for turning against his country.

> He spoke not of the decline of the West, but of its death by greed and constipation. He hated America very deeply ... He also took it for granted that secret services were the only real measure of a nation's political health, the only real expression of its sub-conscious.[40]

I have heard a former Chief of the SIS say on more than one occasion that the British secret services and their operations are 'the last redoubt of our national sovereignty'.[41]

Third example, also taken from the mole's fictional soliloquy of betrayal. The mole, (this is the early 1970s), declares

> The political posture of the United Kingdom is without relevance or moral viability in world affairs ... At Oxford, he said, he was genuinely of the right, and in the war, it scarcely mattered where one stood as long as one was fighting the Germans. For a while, after forty-five, he said, he had remained content with Britain's part in the world, till gradually it dawned on him just how trivial this was. How and when was a mystery. In the historical mayhem

of his own lifetime he could point to no one occasion: simply he knew that if England were out of the game, the price of fish would not be altered by a farthing.[42]

In the mid-1990s the intelligence element in what the then Foreign Secretary, Douglas Hurd, had recently called the factors 'which have allowed Britain to punch above its weight in the world',[43] was, to my mind, an increasingly important ingredient as it enabled the UK, through its communications agreements with the United States, to remain one of only three powers with global intelligence reach (the third was Russia – 20 years on China is coming up fast). I mentioned this to a particularly thoughtful SIS officer, as unlike the fictional mole as it is possible to be, who wondered aloud if this might be 'the itch after the amputation'.[44]

Partly because of the richness of British spy fiction, starting at least with Erskine Childers' 1903 classic *The Riddle of the Sands*,[45] the Establishment secret world sub-branch possesses a frisson and, paradoxically, an attention-seeking characteristic all its own. At the Hay Literary Festival in May 2013, John le Carré tore into what he saw as its dangerous seductive power and he placed it firmly inside the wider Establishment theme:

We pretend we haven't got a political establishment – we do have a political establishment. It is mainly public schools. it is mainly 'people like us'. Its spiritual home is the secret world. It is what access you have, what secret committees you sit on, what secrets you are admitted to. This notion that there is an elite of the indoctrinated is very pernicious. This is very widespread, it is the legal establishment, it is the Press. For the people who are brought into the circle, who get the 'touch', if you are not familiar with the secret world, it is a huge buzz. Particularly people entering politics become intoxicated by that 'touch' and it's very easy to sway them.[46]

Interestingly, at that same session at the Hay Festival, John le Carré acknowledged that the vows he took during his own time inside that secret world still held him: 'I know nothing that could now endanger people but when I went into that world I took a simple vow; the deal was never, ever talk about it and I find myself almost physically unable to discuss it'.[47]

The le Carré perception, as it might be called, is a particular problem for hybrids, insider-outsider figures such as the parliamentarians drawn from both Houses who have sat on the UK's oversight body, the Intelligence and Security Committee (ISC) since its creation under the terms of the Intelligence Services Act 1994. The ISC has acquired more powers and greater reach over its 20-year life, not least thanks to the Justice and Security Act 2013 which made it a committee of Parliament (rather than the committee of Parliamentarians it had been before), extended its remit into operational matters (previously it had been confined to priorities, funding and administration). The ISC's original remit allowed it to take evidence from the heads of the secret services in public but it chose not to do so before the passage of the 2013 Act.

Yet when first it did so on 7 November 2013, the styles of questioning pursued by its MPs and peers were derided in some quarters for their lack of bite and rigour.[48] This was not a view I shared. The session placed a good deal of valuable material on-the-record in a way no set of agency heads had been able to do before. Particularly important, in my judgement, were the damage assessments of the Edward Snowden signals and communications intelligence that Sir Iain Lobban (Director of the Government Communications Headquarters), Andrew Parker (Director General of the Security Service) and Sir John Sawers (Chief of the Secret Intelligence Service) were able to place in the public domain.[49] By having to operate, both properly and inevitably, within the inner loop of secrecy *and* in the public sphere, the ISC is in a position where it cannot win in certain patches of thoughtful press and public opinion as well as the rather less thoughtful spheres of the fantasists and the conspiracy theorists for whom the secret world has always been – and will remain – their cherished adventure playground-of-choice. The danger is that any such oversight body may be seen by the sceptical as yet another clever mutation by the Establishment to preserve and protect those most secret inner citadels of the state.

John le Carré is quite right, however. The world he left in 1964[50] has changed a good deal (not least in its being markedly less public school and Oxbridge[51]). But the world of TOP SECRET – CODEWORD and 'STRAPLINE' for the most sensitively sourced material on an immensely tightly drawn circulation list *is* a heady and seductive one. There is a kind of bond among those who have to carry a high proportion of their professionally acquired secrets to the grave. A trace of it even falls upon those who hunt for the declassifiable residue when, as an Intelligence historian, you mine a newly exposed seam of old – and now safe – files at The National Archives. Whether one is a historian at Kew, a newly appointed

Secretary of State on the inner ministerial intelligence loop or a young Intelligence officer indoctrinated for the first time into that world of codewords and straplines, it's best not to inhale – to resist the mystique which is rarely a problem if you work for the Department of Work and Pensions in a Benefit Office (which is not to demean the importance of serving in the engine room of the welfare state).

A highly and widely experienced friend, who kindly read the draft text of *Establishment and Meritocracy* for me, said: 'The one thing with which I disagree is the attention you give to the spooks. I don't see them as ever having been part of the Establishment'. Though, he added, the occasional member of the Establishment had been 'parachuted in'. An interesting point from a seasoned insider. But John le Carré is on to something – maybe the secret world should be seen as a separate Establishment that until the 1989 Security Service Act and the 1994 Intelligence Services Act dare not – did not – speak its name as a deniable part of the UK's peacetime secret state.

John le Carré is also right in that Establishment membership is a state-of-mind as much as anything else – and this applies to whatever institution or profession you belong to. Rarely these days is it a state-of-dress (a generation ago a very senior and accomplished diplomat could be brilliantly described as fielding 'perhaps one pinstripe too far.'[52])

Naturally, those who play – or have played – in the Establishment's equivalent of the Premier League and very visibly so, have a tendency to resent the very notion more powerfully than anyone else but for reasons of camouflage, or self-image rather than class motivations or social and professional envy. For example, that great lawyer, Cyril Radcliffe, was profoundly irritated by the Establishment idea. Writing in 1961, when the satire boom – *Beyond the Fringe* and all that – was getting going, he said:

> Let a fairy grant me my three wishes, I would gladly use them all in one prayer only, that never again should anyone using pen or typewriter be permitted to employ that inane cliché 'Establishment'.[53]

I fear Lord Radcliffe, up there in the Supreme Court-in-the-sky, is doomed to disappointment. We Brits will never give up on the Establishment as a notion. It's deep within us. As a theme it's had more comebacks than the Rolling Stones. For all the angry words, the denunciations, the parodies and the conspiracy theories we nurture it – almost cherish it. Why? Because quite apart from the fun of trying to determine who is or isn't in it in each generation, it brings fascination to the curious, a target for venting and, therefore, catharsis to the resentful and stimulus to the conspiracy theorist. The British Establishment, like that great cathedral of a British Constitution which it serves as a kind of flying buttress, is Cobbett's 'Thing'. But it's also a thing of magic, mystery, curiosity and fantasy (of which more later).

The Power of a Word

If I were to attempt a volume of 'Establishment studies' it would be suffused, too, by the twin theme of meritocracy. I first felt its punch not in Michael Young's pages (that came later) but in Anthony Sampson's second *Anatomy*. There it was, 'meritocracy', with its attendant, fissile formula:

$$IQ + EFFORT = MERIT.$$

As a grammar schoolboy, a bit of a swot (though I tried zealously to conceal it) and a classic product of Rab Butler's 1944 Education Act, I smelt not a whiff of anything wrong with that equation. For me it was a manifesto and a self-evident truth rather than a warning of what an unbridled pursuit of meritocracy could do.

Not until I finally read Michael Young's classic 1958 fusion of historical sociology, satire, futurology and prediction in *The Rise of the Meritocracy*, did I really inhale the fact that this was a warning – that Young was foreseeing another and, once established, irreversible social and economic deprivation that would (my words; not Young's) rank alongside William Beveridge's famous 'five giants on the road to reconstruction' of his eponymous November 1942 report on social insurance – Ignorance, Idleness, Disease, Squalor and Want.[54]

For Young did see the possible rise of a society which

valued intelligence above all other characteristics as a giant blemish – a society in which the intellectual haves regard the also-rans and the have-nots with disdain and without a trace of the *noblesse oblige* or compassion that had mitigated some of the worst effects of the *ancien régime* of an aristocracy based on blood and inherited wealth rather than the little grey cells. If we could rise – have risen – by our own efforts, hoist upwards by our synapses, so could they if they put their minds to it now that higher education is increasingly available; that was the meritocrats' cry.

The thought occurs that *The Rise of the Meritocracy* might have been Young's way of projecting his 1950s thinking about family and kinship on to a national, a British scale through the medium of educational opportunity and reward. Could it be that Young, like George Orwell in his great 1940 essay, *The Lion and the Unicorn*, saw our country as 'a family with the wrong members in control'?[55] Certainly he foresaw the wrong mix at the top in the new Establishment that would be created once the meritocracy in his fictional treatment of the post-1958 era had risen: A society lacking a sense of natural familyhood or real kinship between the meritocratic possessors and those they regarded as laggards or dullards.

Young does not draw directly on Orwell in *The Rise of the Meritocracy*. But there is one thinker/writer with a special eye for his country who suffuses Young's pages. For Young's dystopic vision is partly built on the analysis of his great hero, the saintly economic and social historian, RH Tawney, in *his* classic work *Equality*, first written in 1931 and updated in 1952. Tawney believed that deep in our collective make-up as a country there was a potent, trumping ingredient – a powerful, British impulse towards inequality. Tawney liked to quote Matthew Arnold on the capacity of we Brits to worship a kind of 'Religion of Inequality'.[56] I think this is much diminished in the 21st century, not for reasons of social solidarity, as Tawney would have wished, but because of anger directed, sometimes indiscriminately, at a variety of targets – for example, bankers post the great crash of 2008 and Etonian 'toffs' in the Cabinet Room following the general election of 2010.

One of Tawney's multiple prescriptions for a better society was ever-improving education for all – a view Michael Young, naturally, shared in full. But he took a step further than Tawney in *The Rise*, as I'll call the book for short. Young, in the historical section of the book, with that gift for epigram he possessed, had summed up the long, grinding and never entirely complete shift from feudalism to capitalism, in these words:

the soil grows castes; the machine makes classes.[57]

Such a society, Young argued, was used to social stratification, so that when the meritocracy rose it was content, for a time, that a new form of stratification had usurped the old,[58] in response to the imperatives of witnessing in the mid to late 1950s a trading nation and slipping former great power in the world plumping for the unleashing of a full throttle, unashamed meritocracy as a way of coping with the global competition and reversing relative economic decline. It was, though Young did not put it this way, a matter of merit or die.

His argument was that economic and competitive pressures would finally force the UK to end what Young called '[t]he perpetual struggle between kinship and merit in favour of merit'. The old class system with its inefficiencies, absurdities and injustices would be swept away only to replace an aristocracy of birth with a meritocracy of talent that would, unlike the old 'ocracy' it was killing off, be both unreformable and irreversible until, that is, the riots and social disturbances of 2034 with which the *Rise* ends and during which Michael Young's *alter ego*, the narrator, the social analyst of the book in whom Young places his thoughts and words, is killed – the moral being that all seemingly triumphant 'ocracies', like all empires, light a fuse beneath themselves.

Michael Young, I'm sure, was deadly serious in writing *The Rise*. But he also had fun along the way. When I reread the book in 2013, I jotted down a few of the forecasts about Britain and the world 1958–2034 that he foresaw happening. Here they are in no particular chronological order or order of magnitude. Some happened; some didn't; some still might happen:

+ The rise of China.
+ A daily shuttle from Earth to the Moon.
+ The UK becoming a province of Europe.
+ The rise of computers and artificial intelligence.
+ A growing North-South divide within the UK.
+ The rise of automation in industry and commerce and, with it, technological redundancy among the workforce.
+ A widespread return of domestic service.

- The end of hereditary peerages with the House of Lords (which Michael himself joined as Lord Young of Dartington in 1977) transformed into a citadel of meritocracy and the chamber in which the Prime Minister sits.
- Together the meritocratised House of Lords and the meritocratic career Civil Service would dominate a deteriorating, though elected, House of Commons.
- A discovered ability to control the weather, for example, to bring on autumn early.

The Rise of the Meritocracy is, in a strange way, literally a touchstone book. Historians, social scientists, commentators and politicians go back and touch it, consult it, when they try to make sense of the vectors, forces and contingencies as they, for better or worse, play out. The legs *The Rise* has acquired over the years since 1958 are all the more remarkable because, as Michael Young wrote in the 'Introduction' to a new 1994 edition:

For some years I thought the book was doomed never to appear. I hawked it round from one publisher to another – eleven of them – and was always turned down ... It was finally published at all because I happened to meet an old friend, Walter Neurath, on a beach in North Wales. He and his wife, Eva, started a publishing house, Thames and Hudson, which has become highly renowned on both sides of the Atlantic for its books on the arts. Sociology was not among its interests; Neurath published my book out of friendship.[59]

'Soon after the book was first published', Young went on, 'it was taken up by Penguin and sold hundreds of thousands of copies, as well as appearing in seven translations. I have sometimes wondered', said Young, 'what on earth Japanese readers make of it'.

Catching a Mood

In that same 1994 'Introduction', Michael Young was interesting on why *The Rise* 'should ... have caught on?' 'It must', he concluded,

> have been partly the title. I had doubts about the key word which I made up. A friend, a classical scholar, said I would be breaking the rules of good usage to invent a new word out of one Latin and one Greek word. I would, she said, be laughed to scorn if I did. In the event the book has been subjected to much criticism but not on grounds of bad taste about the title – rather the opposite, I would say.[60]

Why did Young believe this? Because, he reflected,

The twentieth century had room for the word. People of power and privilege were readier than ever to believe that modern society (in the language of the book) has 'rule not so much by the people as by the cleverest people; not an aristocracy of birth, not a plutocracy of wealth, but a true meritocracy of talent'. The association with the aristocracy was particularly formidable. Some people like to congratulate themselves on being like aristocrats but going one better by earning power and privilege on merit. Aristocracy went wrong because so many of the people who had power simply because they inherited it from their parents were clearly unfit to exercise it. Nobody should be born with a silver spoon in their mouth, or, if he is, it should choke him.[61]

There was another reason, I think, why *The Rise* caught a mood. It was because Michael Young's friend, the great American sociologist, Daniel Bell, and others were proclaiming (wrongly, as it turned out) that the globe was being reshaped by the 'end of ideology', and being made increasingly safe for the ever more indispensable gifted and technocratic.

I shall return to Daniel Bell shortly. *The Rise* certainly attracted attention as soon as it was published from Young's peers and intellectual contemporaries. His friend Noel Annan (himself no mean historical sociologist) wrote a book about his and Michael's generation which he called *Our Age*, published in 1990. Thirty years earlier, Annan recalled, the confident virtues of the post-1944 Butler Act system – of schooling divided into grammar and secondary moderns with a thin sprinkling of technical schools scattered among them – were fraying a little at the edges.

'By the late Fifties', wrote Noel Annan,

the soul of justice awoke from its slumbers. A few dons were asking who had benefitted from Butler's Act. A young Cambridge economist, John Vaizey, turned himself into an expert on the economies of education. He found the ministry of education deficient in the most elementary statistics, and his work showed that Britain was spending a lower proportion of its national income on education than it did in the depths of the Depression in the thirties. Jean Floud showed that the successful children in secondary schools were those who had literate parents; David Glass and Richard Titmuss at LSE that the main beneficiaries of the Butler Act – even of the welfare state – were the middle classes.[62]

This was the sociological and analytical climate into which *The Rise* emerged – its impact all the greater because it was written as a rattling good story, shot through with satire, and built around a paradox – the indispensable need for a society and an economy powered by brains yet in danger of ceasing to be a decent society in the very process and all in the name of social advance.

'Suddenly', wrote Noel Annan, 'the very notion of meritocracy, an elite, began to be attacked. In 1958 Michael Young wrote a book that caught the imagination of Our Age. In *The Rise of the Meritocracy* he imagined what would happen when academic and intellectual merit was the acknowledged criterion for all posts and jobs, from prime minister to dustman. By 2033 everything had gone according to plan but unaccountably the workers began to rebel'.[63]

The excluded, the non-meritorious losers amongst the unskilled male work force allied with clever, radical, women graduates form the Populist Party, a grouping Young's narrator in *The Rise* does not take seriously when writing his great essay in 2033. Anticipating the planned rally in Manchester at Peterloo – the very same site as the great rising in 1819 in May 2034, Young's essayist ventures his own forecast:

Behind the shift and turn of current politics is the underlying fact with which I opened my essay. The last century has witnessed a far-reaching redistribution of ability between the classes in society, and the consequence is that the lower classes no longer have the power to make revolt effective. For a short moment they may prosper through an alliance with the odd and passing disillusion of a section of the upper classes. But such *déclassé* people can never be more than an eccentric minority – the Populists have never been more than that as a serious political force – because the elite is treated with all the wise distinction that any heart can desire. Without intelligence in their heads, the lower classes are never more menacing than a rabble ...

If the hopes of some earlier dissidents had been realized and the brilliant children from the lower classes remained there, to teach, to inspire, and to organize the masses, then I should have had a different story to tell. The few who now propose such a radical step are a hundred years too late. This is the prediction I shall expect to verify when I stand next May listening to the speeches from the great rostrum at Peterloo.[64]

So end the words of Young's essayist/narrator – champion and historian of the risen meritocracy.

But the book finally finishes brilliantly and unforgettably with a footnote:

Since the author of this essay was himself killed at Peterloo, the publishers regret they were not able to submit to him the proofs of his manuscript, for the corrections he might have wished to make before publication. The text, even this last section, has been left exactly as he wrote it. The failings of sociology are as illuminating as its successes.[65]

Michael Young, with that ending, leaves his story, the notion of meritocracy and us – his readers – up in the air. Deliberately so. And successive commentators, who have used the book over the 56 years since it hit the shelves, have been floating atop its paradoxes too. Young would, I think, have been pleased by that. Why? Because in his 1994 reflection he recognised that the growth of mass educational provision had been 'one of the most significant phenomena' of the twentieth century, that a 'basic education has been regarded as a universal right' and that '[i]f there has to be selection at some rung on the educational ladder (as there always has to be), selection should surely not be on the basis of the parents' position or wealth but according to the merit of the child or youth' – that '[p]ractically and ethically, a meritocratic education underpins a meritocratic society'.[66]

Therefore, as Young wrote in 1994, *The Rise of the Meritocracy* was:

intended to present two sides of the cases – the case against as well as the case for a meritocracy. It is not a simple matter and was not intended to be. The two points of view are contrasted throughout. The imaginary author has a shadow. The decision, one way or another, was, and is, left to the reader, the hope being that, on the way to making up his or her mind on one of the great issues of modern society, he or she will also have a little fun.[67]

Hence the satire.

An Enduring Impact

The book and the 'ocracy' it unleashed upon the world have had – and continue to have – a remarkably percussive effect. *The Meritocracy Quartet*, for example, is the collective name of four novels by Jeffrey Lewis charting the progress of his generation in the United States.[68] The word 'meritocracy' can be dropped into conversation in a way that is easily understood and carries a lot of freight. A couple of personal examples.

Shortly before Christmas 2012 the BBC's Parliament Channel invited Lord Carrington, Bernard Donoughue and myself to take part in a studio discussion titled '*1963 – A Year to Remember*'.[69] At the end, we were each asked to sum up the significance of 1963. Bernard (grammar school, Oxford, Labour peer) said:

> 1963 was the year meritocracy came in, [part of] closing the door on the old and bringing in the new.

Just after Easter 2013, I was underwater aboard a Royal Navy Trafalgar class submarine, *HMS Talent* (a suitable name for a boat crammed with specialist sailors from a multiplicity of backgrounds), somewhere off the Isle of Arran and talking to its direct and energetic captain, Commander John Aitken. What he really liked about the Submarine Service, John said, was that it was a true meritocracy. Your background didn't matter. Whether or not you could do the job was all that counted – a rather crucial point in a trade where any one of the crew can lose the boat and whose unwritten motto is 'we all come back or none of us come back'. The same feeling applies to other callings. One hopes for a meritocracy on the flight deck when flying; in the theatre when being operated upon.

Of course such sentiments as Commander Aitken's were plentiful long before Michael Young coined the word 'meritocracy'. A particularly pleasing and pithy example is Ludwig van Beethoven's formulation. On being asked if the 'van' in his name indicated that he was an aristocrat, the great composer replied, with a touch of acid,

I'm not a landowner. I'm a brain owner.[70]

In Margaret McMillan's marvellous study of the road to 1914, *The War That Ended Peace*, is a telegram drafted by the German Ambassador in London, Count Paul Metternich, for transmission to Berlin in 1903 when the great Dreadnought-driven Anglo-German naval race was getting into its stride:

The least ill humour towards us prevails in the higher circles of society, perhaps also in the lower classes of the population. But all of those that lie in between, and who work with brain and pen, the great majority are hostile to us.[71]

'Meritocrats Against the Kaiser' one might call them.

Michael Young in 1958 drew into a single word a great many ingredients from what Harold Perkin called *The Rise of*

Professional Society[72] in Britain. Formal recognition that the word had arrived, naturally, came from the *Oxford English Dictionary*. I'm taking this from the 1989 edition:

> Meritocracy. Government by persons selected on the basis of merit in a competitive educational system; a society so governed; a ruling or influential class of educated people. First use. Michael Young, *The Rise of the Meritocracy*.[73]

Meritocracy pretty well instantly became one of the qualitative measures of post-1958 British society. As a quantitative indicator, it's more problematic. It would be a brave social scientist who attempted an RMI – a relative meritocracy index – or placed too much weight upon such an indicator even if it was possible to create one.

However, there is a fascinating book to be written, a work of special social cartography mapping meritocracy in Britain since the passage of the 1944 Education Act. I'm not a sociologist or a social scientist by trade or training so I'm not the one to attempt it. But I hope somebody will. There are some natural cartographers of relative equality who are convinced that a good proportion of Michael's fears were realised.

Here, for example, is Roy Hattersley in August 2013 writing in *The Guardian* about 'A book that changed me' – Tawney's *Equality*. 'Some passages in *Equality* entranced me by their majestic certainty', he wrote:

> Fifty years before meritocracy was elevated from Michael Young's satire on selfishness into a social system devoutly to be wished, Tawney [in the 1930s] dismissed equality of

opportunity in two irresistible sentences. 'It is only the presence of a high degree of practical equality which can diffuse and generalise opportunities to rise. The existence of such opportunities ... depends not only on an open road, but upon an equal start'.[74]

It's interesting that Roy Hattersley alights on the 1980s as the hour of meritocracy selfish-version. In Michael Young's speculative forward look, the 1980s were key – though in Young's fantasy it was Croslandite democratic socialists in a future Labour government (people like Roy Hattersley) whom he foresaw as the propellants of the meritocracy/ reversing economic decline school. Instead, it was a succession of Conservative governments fuelled by Mrs Thatcher's free market economic liberalism that set out to do this.

Indeed, the very month the grammar school and Oxford educated lady became Leader of the Conservative Party in February 1975, Margaret Thatcher, speaking to the Young Conservatives' Conference in Eastbourne, placed the principle of meritocracy firmly at the centre of her battle standard. 'I believe', she declared,

we should judge people on merit and not on background. I believe the person who is prepared to work hardest should get the greatest rewards and keep them after tax.[75]

This is exactly what she set out to achieve after crossing the threshold of No. 10 Downing Street in May 1979.

Did the Meritocracy Rise?

This question would surely be central to our scholarly cartographer of meritocracy since 1945. What other ingredients might he or she inject? His or her gaze would certainly need to linger on the 'ocracies' that rose which Michael Young did not foresee. For example, 'celebritocracy' – the famous-for-being-famous phenomenon (which sometimes travels under related 'ti's' as 'glitterati' or the 'flasherati'[76]). Related is the rise of the 'media-ocracy' (if such a word is coinable) with its attendant professions of public relations in all its varieties. Another riser is the consulting profession – political as well as managerial – with all the impoverishment it has inflicted upon the language of politics and government which it would take a George Orwell to map (his 1946 essay on 'Politics and the English Language' remains unsurpassed[77]).

The most difficult task for our scholarly cartographer would be determining where we are now. If one argues that Michael Young was foreseeing the rise of what we would now call the 'knowledge economy' then, in that sense, a meritocracy of the knowledgeable has risen according to figures produced by the Work Foundation covering the past 30 years.

Rise of Knowledge Workers (as a percentage of the UK workforce)
1984: 31%   2014: 45%

Fall of Skilled and Semi-Skilled Workers

1984: 28%   2014: 18%

Fall of Unskilled Workers

1984: 16%   2014: 9%[78]

What have the calibrations of rising meritocracy done to the traditional British measurement of class by occupation? In a word, they have complicated it considerably.

A joint team of social analysts at the London School of Economics and the University of Manchester presented on this theme in a very illuminating fashion at the conference of the British Sociological Association in April 2013. Theirs was a mixture of new and old classes trying to capture, for example, what Professor Fiona Devine of Manchester called a 'much more fuzzy area between traditional working class and traditional middle class'.[79]

The Times newspaper, clearly taken (and so am I) by this new taxonomy of socio-economic-cultural class, produced a very useful summarising graphic for its readers.[80]

The LSE/Manchester taxonomy is streaked with meritocracy rising if not suffused by it. But the most potent associated anxiety in the second decade of 21st century Britain is the pace and degree of social mobility of a country hauling itself out of the protracted post-2008 recession. Such worries kept erupting in different forms. Wasn't the spread of unpaid internships for young graduates across the professions merely a reinforcement of the barrier between already-have and would-like-to-have families? The moment IQ enters the debate, discussion becomes volatile and, when it's the Mayor

Elite (6%)	• Wealthiest and most privileged class • Average age: 57 • Highest for social, cultural and economic factors • Many went to private school and elite universities • Most likely to be found living in London and Home Counties • Exclusive and hard to join. Most members come from privileged backgrounds.
Established middle class (25%)	• Most gregarious and second wealthiest class • Average age: 46 • Enjoy a diverse range of cultural activities • Socialise with a broad range of people • Many work in management or the traditional professions • Most come from middle-class backgrounds • Often live outside urban areas
Technical middle class (6%)	• A small, distinctive and prosperous new class • Average age: 52 • Tend to mix socially with people similar to themselves • Prefer emerging culture, such as using social media, to highbrow culture • Many in research, science and technical occupations • Tend to live in suburban locations, often in South East • They come from largely middle-class backgrounds
New affluent workers (15%)	• Sociable with lots of cultural interests. In the middle in terms of wealth • Average age: 44 • Youthful and economically secure, without being well off • High scores for emerging culture but tend not to favour highbrow culture • Likely to come from a working-class background • Many in old manufacturing centres in the Midlands and North West
Traditional working class (14%)	• Score low for economic, social and cultural factors, but do have some financial security • Average age: 66 • Many own their own home • Tend to mix with people like themselves • Tend not to enjoy emerging culture, such as going to the gym or using social media • Oldest average age • Jobs include lorry drivers, cleaners and electricians
Emergent service workers (19%)	• Financially insecure but score high for social and cultural factors • Average age: 34 • Youngest of all the classes • Highest score for emerging culture, which includes going to gigs, using social media and playing sport • Live in cheap cities such as Liverpool and Newcastle • Broad range of friends • Jobs include chefs and nursing auxiliaries
Precariat (15%)	• Most deprived class. Members score low for economic, social and cultural factors • Average age: 50 • Tend to mix with people like themselves • Jobs include cleaner, van driver and care worker • Tend not to have a broad range of cultural interests • Often live in old industrial areas • More than 80% rent home

of London, Boris Johnson, doing the asserting, inevitably volcanic.

His lecture at the Centre for Policy Studies in memory of Margaret Thatcher on 28 November 2013 reached into a world previously unknown to social analysis – that of the cereal. 'Like it or not', declaimed the Mayor, in a series of staccato paragraphs perhaps more suited to an Oxford Union performance than a lecture,

> the free market economy is the only show in town. Britain is competing in an increasingly impatient and globalised economy, in which the competition is getting ever stiffer.
>
> No one can ignore the harshness of that competition, or the inequality that it inevitably accentuates; and I am afraid that violent economic centrifuge is operating on human beings who are already very far from equal in raw ability, if not spiritual worth.

And here came the passage which both reached for the cereal and lit the blue touch paper:

> Whatever you may think of the value of IQ tests, it is surely relevant to a conversation about equality that as many as 16 per cent of our species have an IQ below 85, while about 2 per cent have an IQ above 130. The harder you shake the pack, the easier it will be for some cornflakes to get to the top.[81]

That same autumn the Organisation for Economic Co-operation and Development (OECD) in Paris published its

Programme For International Student Assessment (PISA) results for 2012. PISA publishes triennially and the 2012 'key findings' stimulated another burst of self-questioning in the UK, particularly these ones:

- The United Kingdom performs around the average in mathematics and reading and above the average in science compared with the 34 OECD countries that participated in the 2012 PISA assessment of 15 year-olds.
- When compared with PISA 2006 and PISA 2009, there has been no change in performance in any of the subjects tested.
- The United Kingdom has a higher GDP and spends more on education than the average in OECD countries, as well as higher levels of tertiary education and a lower share of the most socio-economically deprived groups. However, these comparative advantages do not have a clear relationship with educational outcomes.
- As in many other countries, socio-economically disadvantaged students in the United Kingdom are less likely to succeed at school than their more advantaged peers. However, some countries are more successful than the United Kingdom in reducing the influence of socio-economic status on student performance.[82]

As always in the great UK educational/life chances/social mobility debate, the grammar school question was reprised and flickered vividly for a while because in the last months of 2013, the press, who like nothing better, were able to personalise it as the Mayor of London versus the Chief Education Officer for England, Sir Michael Wilshaw. The Old Etonian Mayor had praised grammar schools in his Margaret Thatcher Lecture:

> She was a grammar schoolgirl herself, and she knew what it was like to be up against the kind of smug, sleek men who never dreamed that she would be Prime Minister, never thought she would have the guts to sack posh public school chaps like them.

A few weeks later, in an interview with the *Observer*, Sir Michael said the remaining 164 grammar schools (there were 1,298 in England at their peak in 1964 when 25.5% of secondary pupils were absorbed by them compared to 5% now) did very little for social mobility as they were 'stuffed full of middle class kids'.[83] It would be absurd, in my view, to expect the small surviving band of grammar schools to be an engine of social advance in 2013 (but a fascinating book could be written about the grammar school beneficiaries of the 1944 Education Act).

In my judgement, by far the most significant analysis of autumn 2013 was the 'State of the Nation' report produced by the Social Mobility and Child Poverty Commission set up by Parliament in the Child Poverty Act 2010 (as amended by the Welfare Reform Act 2012), led by Alan Milburn, an ex-Labour Health Secretary, and Gillian Shephard, a former Conservative Education and Employment Secretary as chair and deputy chair respectively. On the key meritocratic question of 'birth not worth,'[84] as their joint foreword put it, it passed a sober judgement on the accumulated attempts of all governments since the postwar settlement (the 1944 Education Act and the post-1945 welfare reforms). Milburn and Shephard concluded that:

> Despite often considerable effort, social elites have not opened up, whether at top universities or in the top professions ... We see a danger that social mobility – having risen in the middle of the last century then flatlined towards the end – could go into reverse in the first part of this century.[85]

One of their key recommendations of factors that 'can unlock social progress' was 'society becoming less unequal over time and individuals with little wealth being supported to build assets'.[86]

Ferdinand Mount, a former head of Margaret Thatcher's Downing Street Policy Unit, had reached a very similar conclusion a year earlier in his *The New Few*, a study of power and inequality in contemporary Britain. Mount's critique also possessed a Michael Young touch in his concern that growing inequality of incomes in the UK had also led to an 'inequality of respect ... It is only in our own time ... that a sharpening inequality of income has been accompanied by a pervading contempt for those who are at the bottom of the ladder and may have less chance of climbing a few rungs than their parents had – and less inclination to try'.[87] Michael Young, in Mount's judgement, in *The Rise of the Meritocracy*, 'was out to show ... that in a society where all the top places are awarded on merit the losers have no hiding place and no excuses'.[88]

The sharp increase of income inequality in the UK was not, I think, foreseeable in 1961 when *The Rise of the Meritocracy* first appeared in paperback and Harold Macmillan was in Downing Street. The dramatic opening of such a yawning gap, especially after 1979, has added to the scratchiness of British society and filled the pools of its resentments particularly since the financial crash of 2008. I am grateful to Stephen Aldridge, Chief Analyst at the Department for Communities and Local Government, for the graph reproduced here and the Institute for Fiscal Studies on whose figures it rests (it was part of Stephen's presentation to 'The Changing Shape of our Society and Government' session at the Cross-Government Strategic Foresight Symposium held in London on 10 February 2014).

Income, of course, is but one of the criteria for measuring social mobility. A highly successful career in say, public service or teaching, may bring you status but certainly not stratospheric financial reward. To reach their conclusion that social mobility improved in the mid-twentieth century and that it 'has, at best, flatlined more recently',[89] the Social Mobility and Child Poverty Commission's analysts drew, among other sources, on studies of the 1958 and 1970 birth cohorts and a discussion paper on social mobility produced by the Cabinet Office's Performance and Innovation Unit in 2001. The Cabinet Office report examined the question of intergenerational mobility (children's prospects compared to that of their parents) and concluded that:

Inequality between top earners and middle and low income earners has risen

Between 1961 and 2012, the ratio of the incomes of the richest 10% relative to the poorest 10% increased from around 3:1 to over 5:1.

Over the past 30 years, the real incomes of those with median household incomes rose 54% compared with 42% for the bottom 10% and 71% for the top 10%

Source: IFS

there is and continues to be a considerable amount of *absolute* social mobility. Over the long run, increasing numbers of children have enjoyed upward social mobility compared with their parents because economic and social change has increased employment opportunities in the professional classes. There has, in other words, been 'more room at the top'.

But, the Cabinet Office study concluded, 'the growth in the rate of absolute social mobility, especially upward social mobility, appears to have been halted in recent decades', despite that extra room at the top.[90]

The Prototype Meritocracy in Trouble?

Michael Young did not regard the British Civil Service as flawless but he admired it greatly and considered it the UK's first meritocracy whose rise took place from the 1870s when 'patronage [was] at last abolished in the Civil Service and competitive entry made the rule. Merit became the arbiter, attainment the standard, for entry and advancement in a splendid profession'.[91] Young sensed the exemplary potency of the 1854 report on Civil Service recruitment produced by the Permanent Secretary to the Treasury, Sir Charles Trevelyan, and the Conservative politician, Sir Stafford Northcote, which gave WE Gladstone, as Chancellor of the Exchequer and, later, Prime Minister, the instruments he needed to create a modernised, meritocratic machine at the heart of British Government.[92]

Yet at the time of writing (early 2014) there are genuine fears that the Gladstonian settlement – in my view, the greatest single governing gift from the nineteenth to the twentieth and twenty-first centuries – might be about to unravel. The question of the future of the senior Civil Service, one of the grandest of our gyroscopic professions, fuses twin themes of meritocracy and Establishment in a manner that is as intriguing as it is important.

It took Parliament 156 years to enshrine the Northcote-Trevelyan principles in statute in Part 1 of the Constitutional

Reform and Governance Act 2010 which, in Clause 10, covering 'Selections for appointment to the civil service', states that

A person's selection must be on merit on the basis of fair and open competition.[93]

It's particularly ironic, therefore, that its tenets should have been brought into question in 2012, two years after the Government changed in 2010. The *Civil Service Reform Plan* of June 2012, presented to Parliament by the Prime Minister, David Cameron, and the Cabinet Office Minister with day-to-day responsibility for the Civil Service, Francis Maude, declared that 'in order to reflect Ministers' accountability to Parliament for the performance of their departments, we will strengthen their role in both departmental and Permanent Secretary appointments',[94] known in Whitehall by the shorthand of 'ministerial choice'.

This intention, naturally, caused a degree of anxiety within the Civil Service Commission, the body created by Gladstone to nurture and protect the Northcote-Trevelyan nostrums. The Commission's chairman, Sir David Normington, a former Permanent Secretary at the Home Office, began what one might call a rolling conversation with Francis Maude. In the meantime, increased ministerial choice was paused for a year.

In July 2013, the Cabinet Office published a *Civil Service Reform Plan: One Year On Report* which caused a further surge of anxiety about a possible creeping politicisation of the senior Civil Service by announcing the creation of

'Extended Ministerial Offices' – a fusion of the Whitehall Private Office with a variant of the French *cabinet* system. Such EMOs would embrace a mix of career officials, special advisers and experts brought in for their specialist knowledge as temporary civil servants (with the Civil Service Commission involved in specialist appointments at Whitehall director level or above).[95]

In early January 2014, the Civil Service Commission launched a consultation document on its recruitment principles attempting to clarify and refine its procedures while offering options on the degree of involvement by the Prime Minister and Secretaries of State in Permanent Secretary appointments.

The Commission's document contained a strongly worded section raising doubts about the compatibility of the Government's proposal with the meritocratic tenets of Northcote-Trevelyan:

> In our view – and that of our predecessor commissions – merit is best assessed by a process which has independent oversight, is objective and evidence-based. The risk in the Government's proposal is that it could lead to a Secretary of State substituting his or her personal view of merit for the outcome of an independent, objective assessment process. We doubt whether that is compatible with the legal requirement [the Constitutional Reform and Governance Act 2010] and it risks candidates being seen to be appointed on the basis of personal or political patronage.[96]

The whisper in Whitehall was that if the Government could not get its way on permanent secretary appointments they might seek to amend the 2010 Act.

The combination of 'ministerial choice' and the 'Extended Ministerial Offices' risks, in my judgement, an abandonment of the Northcote-Trevelyan principles – and similar fears were widely expressed in a debate on the future of the Civil Service in the House of Lords on 16 January 2014[97] and linked to calls from House of Commons Select Committees for a wider inquiry into the Civil Service.[98]

At the time of writing, all these questions are still in play. But the crucial test of the politicisation question will come on a change of government to another political colour whenever that might be. If greater 'ministerial choice' of permanent secretaries has been put into operation and a swathe of Extended Ministerial Offices created (especially if they have morphed into central directorates; departments within departments), might not the new incoming government – no doubt with expressions of public regret – say we cannot trust these people; they are creatures of the outgoing administration so we must seek bespoke senior civil servants of our own?

Such an outcome, in my judgement, would represent a national own goal of considerable proportions if career civil servants came to be recruited to any serious degree because of the beauty of their political opinions rather than the intellectual and analytical capacities – and increasingly, managerial gifts – they can bring to public service.

The Pursuit of a 'Well-Tempered Meritocracy'

My own view is that those of us who absorbed Michael Young's warning when we were about to scale the first rungs of our own professional ladders were – and remain – riven by the concept of meritocracy. It was a self-evidently worthy impulse but it carried risks of callousness and disdain towards those who did not rise in terms of high status and well paid jobs. What we were seeking, on reflection, was the best of both worlds – what Michael Young's friend, the great American sociologist Daniel Bell, prophet of the 'Post-Industrial Society', called 'a well-tempered meritocracy'[99] (which has a pleasing ring of JS Bach about it). A 'well-tempered meritocracy' would be one in which its beneficiaries rose to infiltrate the old Establishment in all its forms (except the hereditary monarchy) while never forgetting (a) where they had come from, (b) what it had taken by way of public policy and investment to get them there, (c) the need to keep the ladders they had climbed in ever greater repair to enable a still bigger and more accomplished meritocracy to rise after them and, (d) to avoid at all times a creeping inequality of respect falling upon those who did not rise in a similar fashion. As Daniel Bell expressed it, 'a well-tempered meritocracy can be a society if not of equals, then of the just'.[100]

There is a religious aspect, too, to the dark side of meritocracy. As my friend Richard Chartres, the Bishop of London, has pointed out, the 'anchorage' of RH Tawney's notion of equality was his Christian belief 'of a creation of all humans in the image and likeness of God'.[101] Richard outlined his version of what one might call a Christian-tempered meritocracy on 11 December 2013 in an address to a City Livery Company, the Saddlers, to mark the 650th anniversary of their creation. 'Our society', he said, 'is dominated by regulation and technology. We need to re-discover our heart. If we want to avoid moving into a new ice age of humanity we must give more weight to reasons of the heart'.[102]

At the core of the Bishop's address was a passage with a touch of the Michael Youngs:

> It is not difficult to see why we are so keen to widen our knowledge and why we are so little concerned to increase our capacity to love – knowledge translates directly into power; love translates into service.

'One of the modern idols', Richard continued, 'is the IQ – the intelligence quotient ... Fewer people take the heart quotient into account yet Paul's words remain true "knowledge puffs up but love builds up" [1 Corinthians; Chapter Eight; Verse One]'.[103]

A Very British Pursuit

It has been a central theme of this study that Establishment and meritocracy have been bound together increasingly closely in Britain since Rab Butler's Education Bill received royal assent in 1944. But the questions of social mobility and merit are, of course, first order matters. Establishment hunting, that very British pursuit – for all the thrill of the chase about who's in it and who's not – is essentially a fascinating game, but in reality, it is a diversion from the deeper questions of social mobility and the levels of equality achievable in a liberal capitalist economy within an open world trading system. Searching for it – and resenting it – will always, I suspect, remain a very British pastime and each generation will need its anatomists to attempt the near impossible of discovering its core and mapping its mutations; its traditional grand redoubts in the great professions and the risers and entryist individuals and callings on its rim. The Establishment will retain, too, its special talent for fascinating and infuriating in equal measure.

And, I suspect, its configurations will become more elusive as time passes. Its fragmentary nature was, interestingly enough, emphasised by the Prime Minister, David Cameron, when I asked him about it in the autumn of 2013. The conversation ran like this:

PH: Is there such a thing as 'The British Establishment' these days?

DC: Yes. But not in the same way as there used to be. I think there used to be in the sense that there were a certain group of people from particular schools and universities who ran this sort of organisation and that organisation and the other organisation. And, as a result, that was the Establishment. I think now there are lots of establishments. There's an establishment at the top of the media. They are all slightly different, you know.

PH: Not an overarching one anymore?

DC: I don't think so. There are sort of overlapping ones. They all need to be challenged. They all need to open up. They all need to allow people to break through. And there are some that are healthier than others, as it were. But I don't think there is an overarching one in the same way'.[104]

Prime Ministers occupy a special vantage point from which to observe the various establishments in action given that much Establishment effort involves the discreet seeking of influence in high places such as the PM's study in 10 Downing Street.

David Cameron's point about a media establishment is interesting. I think he's right but not in the sense of proprietors or even, in some cases, editors. The real influencers are to be found in the political commentariat. In some generations there is what one might call a top pen amongst them. Peter Jenkins of *The Guardian* was a top pen as was Hugo Young, also, latterly, of *The Guardian* but previously of *The Sunday Times*.

Other key figures in the commentariat establishment

are the talismanic columnists of left and right such as Polly Toynbee of *The Guardian* or Simon Heffer of the *Daily Mail*. Still more come into this particular establishment stockade if you include the running chorus of the BBC Radio 4 *Today* programme presenters and, flying fierce and solo, Jeremy Paxman of BBC2's *Newsnight* until mid-2014, himself a hunter of the Establishment.

This particular citadel also includes BBC Political Editors who have brought extra personality to traditional impartiality – John Cole, Andrew Marr, Nick Robinson. Robert Peston, the BBC's Economics Editor, is undoubtedly inside it, too, if you widen the lens to political economy. As for the great political occasions (whether it be general elections or great funerals), it doesn't work without David Dimbleby – the supreme specialist of transitions.

Between them, the Commentariat Establishment act, as that shrewd observer of Westminster, Norman Shrapnel, once wrote of Parliament, is a kind of 'repertory company, busy dramatizing an era'[105] to help us find our way through dramas and shifting scenes. They, much more than MPs, are now the guides we look to for this.

On the wider front, David Cameron is right to see establishments as more spread and various and harder to pin down with, in my view, less of tone-setting club at the apex than in the now gone era of classic gooder and greaters like Cyril Radcliffe or Oliver Franks. Perhaps, too, establishments have become more porous and meritocratic. On reflection, I should have asked the Prime Minister to elaborate on how to open the range of establishments up, how best to challenge them and for what purpose.

Conceptual Vitality?

For all their inadequacy as tools for social analysis, the idea of Establishment and the aspiration for meritocracy do possess a continuing utility. Certainly the impulse for meritocracy will remain strong not just as an individual motivator for those wishing to rise but also for collective purposes. As Michael Young caught powerfully in *The Rise of the Meritocracy*, economic survival is the spur and will remain so until that glorious time when British industry, British services and British finance find themselves on a golden trajectory of ever waxing innovation, productivity, competitiveness and growth. Until that shining hour, the patron intellect of meritocracy will be the great New Zealand-born physicist, Sir Ernest Rutherford.[106] At a time of funding cuts he called his team together at the renowned Cavendish Laboratory in Cambridge and said: 'We haven't the money, so we've got to think'.[107]

As for the idea of an Establishment, perhaps even in an era when it takes myriad forms and is harder to pin down than ever we need it as part of the way we imagine the United Kingdom. It can also serve as a transmitter of tradition and maybe even a dab of stability by drawing on the wisdom of those with considerable past experience as Establishment elders. We want it to exist – so exist it does. Meritocracy we need as both a balancer to Establishment and as a bringer of a more efficient and productive society in which the capable and the meritorious receive their rewards. But we don't want meritocracy at the price of creating a detached and self-regarding elite insensitive towards those who have not soared up meritocratic ladders of their own.

It is possible that any essay on Establishment and meritocracy is a wasted enterprise – an atavistic fascination for mid-to-late 20th century notions no more than residuals in a very different society. Rory Stewart, that fascinator on the Conservative backbenches in the House of Commons, certainly thinks so having observed closely the contemporary Britain he found after doing intriguing things for the Foreign Office in Afghanistan and Iraq. His explanation for the elusiveness of the Establishment would be that it simply no longer exists, in his own echo of Hugh Thomas' view.

Early in 2013, after 3½ years plus in Parliament, Rory Stewart told *The Guardian's* Decca Aitkenhead, 'in our situation we are all powerless ... we pretend we're run by people. We're not run by anybody. The secret of modern Britain is there is no power anywhere'.[108] Indeed, there are those who think that the Establishment is pretty well reduced to a handful of its dining clubs. Others are convinced that it is still a product of two special breeding grounds in the public schools and the ancient universities. But I think it is not a question of past educational provenance and current dining habits, it is a more kaleidoscopic, meritocratic and fluid phenomenon than such parodies would suggest. To adapt Gertrude Stein on California, there still is some there there.[109] There is life in the twin themes yet.

Notes

1. Peter Hennessy, 'Thoughts on the British Establishment', *The Middle Templar*, Issue 53, Michaelmas 2013, pp.85–7.

2. Mary Douglas, *How Institutions Think* (Syracuse University Press, 1986), p.1.

3. Stanley Martin, *The Order of Merit: One Hundred Years of Matchless Honour* (I.B.Tauris, 2007), pp.3, 23–36.

4. Michael Young, *The Rise of the Meritocracy: An Essay on Education and Equality* (Thames and Hudson, 1958); Pelican edn (Penguin Books, 1961).

5. 'Gabriele Annan', Obituary, *The Times* 2 December 2013.

6. Jeremy Paxman, *Friends in High Places: Who Runs Britain?* (Penguin, 1991).

7. Anthony Sampson, *Anatomy of Britain Today* (Hodder and Stoughton, 1965).

8. Anthony Sampson, *Anatomy of Britain* (Hodder and Stoughton, 1962), p.632.

9. Labour secured an overall majority of five in the general election of 15 October 1964. David Butler, *British General Elections since 1945* (Institute of Contemporary British History/Blackwell, 1989), p.20.

10. Ben Pimlott, *Harold Wilson* (HarperCollins, 1992), p.307.

11. Harold Wilson, *The New Britain: Labour's Plan* (Penguin, 1964), pp.9–15.

12. ML Pearl, *William Cobbett: A Biographical Account of his Life and Times* (OUP, 1953).

13. AJP Taylor, 'Books in General', *The New Statesman and Nation*, 29 August 1953, pp.236–7.

14. *Report Concerning the Disappearance of Two Former Foreign Office Officials*, Cmd 9577 (HMSO, 23 September 1955). See also Christopher Andrew, *The Defence of the Realm: The Authorised History of MI5* (Allen Lane, 2009), pp.424–26, 431.

15. Henry Fairlie, 'Political Commentary', *Spectator*, 23 September 1955, pp.379–80.

16. Peter Hennessy, *The Great and the Good: An Inquiry into the British Establishment* (Policy Studies Institute, March 1986).

17. Ibid, pp.30–52.

18. Hugh Thomas (ed), *The Establishment. A Symposium* (Anthony Blond, 1959). Fairlie's essay appears between pages 191 and 208.

19. Hugh Thomas, *The Suez Affair* (Pelican, 1970). It was first published in 1966.

20. Hugh Thomas, *The Spanish Civil War* (Eyre and Spottiswode, 1961)

21. Thomas (ed), *The Establishment*, p.14.

22. Ibid, p.15.

23. Ibid. Between pages 23 and 48.

24. Ibid, p.15.

25. Letter to the author from Lord Thomas of Swynnerton, 8 January 2014.

26. Kingsley Martin, *The Crown and the Establishment* (Hutchinson, 1962).

27. Ibid, p.86.

28. Vernon Bogdanor, *The Monarchy and the Constitution* (OUP, 1995), pp.97–8; Ben Pimlott, *The Queen: A Biography of Elizabeth II* (HarperCollins, 1996), p.335.

29. Walter Bagehot, *The English Constitution*, first published 1867 (Fontana edn, 1963), p.100.

30. Sampson, *Anatomy of Britain*, p.50.

31. John Rentoul, *Tony Blair, Prime Minister* (Little Brown, 2001), pp.430–45.

32. House of Lords, *Official Report*, 10 April 2013, col.1127.

33. Paxman, *Friends in High Places*, p.314.

34. Private information. It was the author he was wondering about.

35. Rachel Ward, 'Home and Away. I didn't realise how much I'd miss England', *The Spectator*, 23 February 2013.

36. John le Carré, *Call for the Dead*, first published 1961 (Coronet, 1992), p.9.

37. John le Carré, *Tinker Tailor Soldier Spy* (Hodder, 1974).

38. Ibid, pp.112–13.

39. I have Sir Gerry Warner's permission to cite him.

40. Le Carré, *Tinker Tailor Soldier Spy*, p.337.

41. Private information.

42. Le Carré, *Tinker Tailor Soldier Spy*, pp.336–7.

43. Lord Hurd was speaking at Chatham House on 3 February 1993. Elizabeth Knowles (ed), *The Oxford Dictionary of Modern Quotations* (OUP, 2002), p.163.

44. Private information.

45. Erskine Childers, *The Riddle of the Sands: A Record of Secret Service* (Smith, Elder, 1903). Alan Judd, himself an accomplished novelist, describes it as 'arguably the first modern spy story' in his *Mansfield Cumming and the Founding of the Secret Service* (HarperCollins, 1999), p.33.

46. Simon de Bruxelles, 'Le Carré: secret courts will be a stain on our society', *The Times*, 1 June 2013.

47. Ibid.

48. For example, see 'Intelligence and Transparency. Nothing to See Here'. Leading article, *The Guardian*, 8 November 2013.

49. Intelligence and Security Committee of Parliament, 'Transcript of Evidence', Thursday 7 November 2013 (Stationery Office, 2013).

50. 'David John Moore Cornwell', *Who's Who 2014* (A&C Black, 2013), p.503.

51. This is from private observation rather than data (which does not exist in the public domain).

52. Private information.

53. Lord Radcliffe, 'Censors', The Rede Lecture, University of Cambridge, 4 May 1961. Reproduced in Lord Radcliffe, *Not in Feather Beds* (Hamish Hamilton, 1968), pp.161–82. This particular quotation is on p.175.

54. *Social Insurance and Allied Services, Report by Sir William Beveridge*, Cmd 6404 (HMSO, 1942), p.6.

55. Peter Davison (ed), *Orwell's England* (Penguin, 2001), p.264.

56. RH Tawney, *Equality*, 1952 edn (Unwin Books, 1964), p.33.

57. Young, *The Rise of the Meritocracy*, Pelican edn, p.24.
58. Ibid, p.123.
59. Michael Young, *The Rise of the Meritocracy: With a new introduction by the author* (Transaction Publishers, 1994), p.xi.
60. Ibid, p.xii.
61. Ibid, pp.xii–xiii.
62. Noel Annan, *Our Age. Portrait of a Generation* (Weidenfeld, 1990), p.363.
63. Ibid.
64. Young, *The Rise of the Meritocracy*, Pelican edn, pp.189–90.
65. Ibid, p.190.
66. Young, *The Rise of the Meritocracy*, Transaction edn, pp.xiii-xiv.
67. Ibid, p.ix.
68. Jeffrey Lewis, *The Meritocracy Quartet* (Haus Publishing, 2011).
69. It was shown several times on the Parliament Channel throughout 2013.
70. Quoted by Simon Russell Beale in *Symphony*, BBC 4, 31 May 2013.
71. Margaret McMillan, *The War That Ended Peace: How Europe Abandoned Peace for the First World War* (Profile, 2013).
72. Harold Perkin, *The Rise of the Professional Society: England since 1880* (Routledge, 1989).
73. *Oxford English Dictionary*, Second Edn, Vol.9 (Clarendon Press, 1989), p.635.

74. Roy Hattersley, 'A book that changed me', *The Guardian*, 15 August 2013.

75. Charles Moore, *Margaret Thatcher. The Authorized Biography. Volume One: Not For Turning* (Allen Lane, Penguin Press, 2013), p.294.

76. I am grateful to my friend and former student, Mark Fox, for 'flasherati'.

77. Peter Davison (ed), *Orwell and Politics* (Penguin, 2001), pp.397–410.

78. *Defining the Knowledge Economy* (Work Foundation, 2006).

79. Jack Malvern, 'We know our place in modern Britain, and it's no longer where it used to be', *The Times*, 4 April 2013.

80. Ibid.

81. The Boris Johnson CPS Speech was reproduced in full on *The Daily Telegraph* website, http://www.telegraph.co.uk/news/politics/london-mayor-election/mayor-of-london.10

82. http://www.oecd.org/pisa/keyfindings/pisa-2012-results-htm

83. Daniel Boffey, 'Ofsted chief declares war on grammar schools', *Observer*, 15 December 2013; for a good encapsulation of the ensuing debate see Philip Collins, 'A History Boys education is not for everyone', *The Times*, 20 December 2013. For grammar school statistics 1947–2012 see Paul Bolton, *Grammar School Statistics* (House of Commons Library, 20 May 2013)

84. Social Mobility and Child Poverty Commission, *State of the Nation 2013: social mobility and child poverty in Britain* (TSO, October 2013), p.1.

85. Ibid, pp.4–5.

86. Ibid, p.2.

87. Ferdinand Mount, *The New Few or A Very British Oligarchy: Power and Inequality in Britain Now* (Simon and Schuster, 2012), p.257.

88. Ibid, p.256.

89. Simon Blake, email to the author, 6 January 2014.

90. *Social Mobility. A Discussion Paper* (Performance and Innovation Unit, Cabinet Office, April 2001).

91. Young, *The Rise of the Meritocracy*, Pelican edn, p.19.

92. The Northcote-Trevelyan Report is most easily consulted by turning to the back of the 1968 Fulton Report, *The Civil Service*, Cmnd 3638, Volume I, Appendix B. For its genesis see Peter Hennessy, *Whitehall* (Pimlico edn, 2001), pp.30–51.

93. Constitutional Reform and Governance Act 2010, Part 1, chapter 1, clause 10 (2).

94. *Civil Service Reform Plan* (Cabinet Office, June 2012), p.21

95. *Civil Service Reform Plan: One Year On Report* (Cabinet Office, July 2013), p.31.

96. *Review and Updating of Recruitment Principles: A Consultation* (Civil Service Commission, January 2014), pp.8–9.

97. House of Lords, *Official Report*, Thursday 16 January 2014, cols.354–92.

98. House of Commons Public Administration Select Committee, *Truth to power: how civil service reform can succeed*, HC 74 (Stationery Office, 3 September 2013); House of Commons Liaison Committee, *Civil Service: lacking capacity* (HV 884, (Stationery Office, 12 December 2013).

99. Daniel Bell, *The Coming of Post-Industrial Society: A Venture in Social Forecasting* (Heinemann Educational Book, 1974), p.455.

100. Ibid.

101. Richard Chartres to Peter Hennessy, 21 December 2013.

102. The Rt Reverend Rt Hon Richard Chartres, Address of the Saddlers' Company, 11 December 2013.

103. Ibid.

104. Conversation with David Cameron, 10 Downing Street, 3 October 2013.

105. Norman Shrapnel, *The Performers: Politics at Theatre* (Constable, 1978), p.9.

106. Rutherford, Ernest, Baron (1871–1937), *Oxford Dictionary of Science* (OUP, 2010), p.724.

107. http://www.bl.uk/onlinegallery/features/beautifulminds/learning.html

108. Decca Aitkenhead, 'Anyone running a small pizza business has more power than me,' *The Guardian*, 4 January 2014.

109. She is thought to have said of California 'There's no there there'.

By the same Author

States of Emergency
(with Keith Jeffery)

Sources Close to the Prime Minister
(with Michael Cockerell and David Walker)

What the Papers Never Said

Cabinet

Ruling Performance
(edited with Anthony Seldon)

Whitehall

Never Again: Britain 1945–51

The Hidden Wiring: Unearthing the British Constitution

Muddling Through: Power, Politics and the Quality of
Government in Postwar Britain

The Prime Minister: The Office and Its Holders since 1945

The Secret State: Whitehall and the Cold War

Having It So Good: Britain in the Fifties

The New Protective State: Government, Intelligence and
Terrorism (editor)

Cabinets and the Bomb

The Secret State: Preparing for the Worst, 1945–2010

Distilling the Frenzy:
Writing the History of One's Own Times